HEADSTART HISTORY

Norman Kingship

by

Emma Mason

HEADSTART HISTORY

Published by   HEADSTART HISTORY
                      PO Box 41, Bangor, Gwynedd, LL57 1SB

Set by   C.B.S.
                      155 Hamilton Road,
                      Felixstowe, Suffolk, IP11 7DR

Printed by   THE IPSWICH BOOK COMPANY LTD
                      The Drift, Nacton Road,
                      Ipswich, Suffolk IP3 3QR

ISBN   1 873041 45 4

A CIP catalogue record for this book is available from the British Library.

CONTENTS

Introduction

Further Reading
Bibliography of Emma Mason

Frontispiece :   British Library Royal MS 14C VII f8v :
the Norman Kings and Stephen.
By kind permission of the British
Library

INTRODUCTION

The HEADSTART HISTORY PAPERS aim to identify themes and topics the significance of which extends beyond the studies of professional historians. The PAPERS are distillations of the research of distinguished scholars in a form appropriate to students and the general reader.

Norman Kingship examines the challenges, achievements and the basis of power of rulers from William I to Stephen - men who were threatened by rivals for their throne, by fear of financial disaster, by treachery within their kingdom and by challenge from abroad. To survive all of this they needed to be men of exceptional ability and resourcefulness, and with remarkable strength of character. Their rule was tough and disobedience of the government brought a harsh response. Their power, under-pinned by an image of kingship, was most potent through its links with the church and the symbolism of the coronation. Dr. Mason examines the ambitions of these kings and the con-straints upon them, and she considers their methods of govern-ment. She looks at the aura of kingship and the manner in which the Norman kings exercized their power.

Norman links with England before 1066 are better known to scholars than to the general reader but for everyone the year 1066 has importance for the formal claim - by William, duke of Normandy - to the throne of Edward the Confessor. The Battle of Hastings, the death of Harold and victory of William the Conqueror are embroidered into the Bayeux Tapestry and recorded in chronicles. The Norman military might is still with us in their awesome castles. The Norman kings have also made a deep personal impact. Dr. Mason cites Michael Clanchy:

> "the personal names of the men of the ruling Norman dynasty quickly became the most popular ones bestowed on their English subjects. And since

the single most common recorded name was William, this reflects something of the stature of those kings as perceived by their people".

The greatness of the Norman kings has not been diminished by the passage of time. In fact, increasing knowledge has enhanced our admiration of their achievements and the manner in which they approached every challenge.

Dr. Emma Mason is Reader in Medieval History at Birkbeck College, London. Her scholarship is reflected in her numerous articles, which have appeared in publications such as the *Proceedings of the Battle Conference on Anglo-Norman Studies*; *Studies in Church History*, and the *Journal of Medieval History*. In 1980 she published *The Beauchamp Cartulary: charters 1100-1268* (Pipe Roll Society, Vol. 43) and in 1988 she published *Westminster Abbey Charters, 1066-1214*. (London Record Society, vol. 25). Her most recent book is *St Wulfstan of Worcester, c. 1008-1095*. Dr. Mason has published many articles on English religious and social history, concentrating on the "small worlds" of Westminster Abbey and Worcester Cathedral Priory. She has also examined the development of royal and baronial propaganda. Details of all of these are in the bibliography of her work.

HEADSTART HISTORY has many reasons to be grateful to Dr. Mason since she regularly attends the medieval conferences; has contributed to MONASTIC STUDIES and has also been an enthusiastic supporter and contributor to MEDIEVAL HISTORY, the journal which was launched in January 1991.

I record my warm appreciation to Dr. Mason for writing the first of the medieval HEADSTART HISTORY PAPERS and for the generous way in which she has offered her time and expertise in so many of my projects.

Judith Loades, Bangor, August 1991

NORMAN KINGSHIP

I

This survey of Norman kingship encompasses the reign of William I (1066-1087) those of his two youngest sons, William Rufus (1087-1100) and Henry I (1100-1135), and that of Stephen (1135-1154), the son of William I's daughter Adela. Stephen was a younger son of the comital house of Blois, but he is conventionally considered as the last of the 'Norman' kings - if only because there is no other convenient slot into which he can be fitted. Moreover, he depicted himself as a Norman king in order to reinforce his claim to the throne, as his charters occasionally refer to him as the nearest male heir of his predecessor, 'my uncle, King Henry.'[1] Of these four kings only William Rufus could claim unequivocally to be the choice of his predecessor.[2] William I's similar claim is hedged by doubts regarding both the historical sources and the technicalities of English law,[3] while both Henry I and Stephen seized the throne in the face of rivals. In the face of endemic threats to their authority, the Norman kings were strong and stern rulers. Stephen, the

---

1 For example *Regesta Regum Anglo-Normannorum 1066-1154,* III, ed. H.A. Cronne and R.H.C. Davis (Oxford, 1968), nos. 678-81 (granted to Reading Abbey, founded by Henry I).

2 Frank Barlow, *William Rufus* (London, 1983), 46-7.

3 Ann Williams, 'Some Notes and Considerations on problems connected with the English Royal Succession, 860-1066', *Proceedings of the Battle Conference on Anglo-Norman Studies I. 1978*, ed. R. Allen Brown (Woodbridge, 1979), 165-7.

quasi-Norman, was not, and lived to repent the conse-
quences.

The Norman kings of England, like almost all contem-
porary Continental rulers, and most of their predecessors
in England and elsewhere, faced a series of challenges,
whether from rivals for their own throne; from antago-
nistic rulers of other lands; from treachery at home, or
from the fear that their revenues were inadequate for the
tasks in hand. Much effort had to be made to bolster
their position against such assaults.

II

European rulers traditionally projected themselves as being
set apart from, and above, their subjects, as one way of
combating the potential threat of rebellion. They claimed
that special attributes were bestowed on them at their
king-making - notably by their sacring, anointing with
consecrated oil, and by their crowning.[4] Before 1066 William the Conqueror, as duke of Normandy, was exalted
in a local version of the *Laudes Regiae*, the ceremonial
acclamation traditionally reserved for a king or an em-
peror, an indication of the strength and autonomy of the
duchy.[5] But his anointing and coronation as king of England raised him to a higher plane. The anointing of a
king, on his head, resembled the unction bestowed on a

---

4 Carolly Erickson, *The Medieval Vision: essays in History and
Perception* (Oxford, 1976), 129.

5 H.E.J. Cowdrey, *Popes, Monks and Crusaders* (London, 1984),
VIII 37-78.

bishop, whereas a priest was anointed only on his hands. A king, like a cleric, communicated at the mass in both bread and wine, and the symbolism of king-making made it possible to project kings as wonder-workers.[6]

When each of the four Norman kings made his bid to secure the throne of England, he quickly secured coronation, in order to stabilize his political position, although William the Conqueror was more immediately concerned to ensure the military submission of the English and delayed the completion of his king-making until he had done so.[7] Since Harold Godwinson had undoubtedly been consecrated king, this caused some perplexity to Norman propagandists,[8] but William the Conqueror vindicated his own claim by pointing to the judgement of God in the outcome of the battle 'of Hastings.' Military victory; lack of any further convincing rival, and coronation by the statesmanlike Archbishop Ealdred of York (rather than by the schismatic Stigand of Canterbury) secured the throne for William the Conqueror. In 1087 he chose as his own successor his second surviving son, William Rufus, rather than the rebellious Robert Curthose. Even so, Archbishop Lanfranc was allotted the responsibility of making the final pronouncement on the

---

6 Erickson, *The Medieval Vision*, 129, 133.

7 George Garnett, 'Coronation and Propaganda: some implications of the Norman claim to the throne of England in 1066', *Transactions of the Royal Historical Society*, fifth series, 36 (1986), 92-3.

8 *Ibid.*,98. On the validity of Harold's consecration, see also Janet L. Nelson, *Politics and Ritual in early medival Europe* (London, 1986), 393-5.

succession.[9] In August 1100, Henry I was able to seize the throne simply by being present when his crusading elder brother was absent. His coronation was hurried on, despite the absence of Archbishop Anselm, to whom he later sent perfunctory excuses.[10] Similarly, Stephen seized the throne in the absence both of Henry's designated heir, his daughter Matilda, and also that of the magnates' choice, Stephen's elder brother, Count Theobald of Blois. Stephen's bid for the throne is thought to have owed its success to his brother, Henry of Blois, the bishop of Winchester, who also stage-managed the Empress Matilda's recognition as Lady of the English in 1141. Bishop Henry, together with Archbishop Theobald, later played a leading role in the negotiations between King Stephen and Henry of Anjou in 1153. It is little wonder that one of the Henry of Blois plaques, the surviving fragments of one of his splendid liturgical commissions, carries this inscription: 'May the angel take the giver to Heaven, but not just yet, in case England groans for it, since it depends on him for peace or war, turmoil or rest.'[11]

William Rufus, the designated heir of his father, was consecrated by Lanfranc and obtained oaths of loyalty from all the magnates before proceeding to scrutinize the treasury.[12] Both Henry I and Stephen prudently secured

9 Barlow, *William Rufus*, 55-7.

10 *English Historical Documents 1042-1189*, ed. D.C. Douglas and G.W. Greenaway (London, 1981), 722-3, no. 108.

11 G. Zarnecki, J. Holt and T. Holland (eds.), *English Romanesque Art 1066-1200* (London, 1984), 261.

12 Barlow, *William Rufus*, 63.

the royal treasury at Winchester before proceeding to the formalities of king-making.[13] The royal finances needed to be in a healthy state for any man hoping to convey credibility as a strong ruler. William the Conqueror and his sons understood this, hence their successful campaigns, both in Britain and in defence of their Continental inheritance. Stephen dispersed his resources without due thought for replenishing them, a major contribution to the failures of his reign.[14]

The coronation of William the Conqueror bestowed on him the legitimacy which ratified his share-out of the spoils of victory.[15] From his point of view, his king-making ensured the loyalty of the major English churchmen and forestalled any attempt by insurgents to rally round some rival contender for the throne.[16] English prelates, imbued with the precepts of the *Regularis Concordia*, the basis of the monastic reform of the mid tenth century, were then bound to render the loyalty due to the anointed king.[17] Elements of this particular ideal survived

---

13 R.H.C. Davis, *King Stephen 1135-1154* (third ed., Harlow, 1990), 16. On Henry I, see C. Warren Hollister, *Monarchy, Magnates and Institutions in the Anglo-Norman World*, (London, 1986), 64-5.

14 J.O. Prestwich, 'War and Finance in the Anglo-Norman State', *Transactions of the Royal Historical Society*, fifth series, 4 (1954), 19-43.

15 Garnett, 'Coronation and Propaganda', 93.

16 Pauline Stafford, *Unification and Conquest: a political and social history of England in the tenth and eleventh centuries* (London, 1989), 104.

17 *Regularis Concordia: The Monastic Agreement*, transl. and ed. T. Symons (London, 1953), 12-14, 16, 20-23.

the Normanization of the English monasteries. Archbishop Lanfranc, in his *Monastic Constitutions,* instructed the monks of Canterbury cathedral priory to genuflect to the king, as they would to abbots or to the pope.[18]

Norman monasteries welcomed the triumph of William I, which was expected to enhance his rule in the duchy, and thereby reinforce the protection which he could afford them against predatory laymen. At Easter 1067 his ducal monastery of Fecamp organized a splendid version of the *Laudes Regiae.* In Normandy such rituals were performed before a monastic, or at any rate a clerical congregation. In England, on the other hand, the *Laudes* were celebrated before mixed assemblies of notables, starting with the consecration of William's wife Matilda as queen, on 11 May 1068. The *Laudes Regiae* drew an analogy between the heavenly hierarchy and that on earth - in which the king was prominently named. This ritual used in 1068 was possibly composed by the English Archbishop Ealdred of York, who had travelled extensively in German territory on diplomatic embassies. The influence of the German *Laudes Regiae* can be discerned in the English ritual of 1068, indicating that William's new royal status was enhanced by emulation of the prestigious German imperial ritual, rather than that of the weaker Capetian kings.[19] The *Laudes Regiae* of the German, French and English courts ultimately derived their

---

18 *Decreta Lanfranci: The Monastic Constitutions of Lanfranc,* transl. and ed. D. Knowles (London, 1951), 70-2, 74.

19 Nelson, *Politics and Ritual in early medieval Europe,* 396-8. See also Cowdrey, *Popes, Monks and Crusaders,* 37-78.

inspiration from the triumphal victory ceremonies of the late Roman world, which were later developed as propaganda exercizes, and transmitted through the Byzantine empire to the Carolingian rulers.[20]

In England, the *Laudes* Regiae, popularly known from their opening words as the *Christus Vincit* (Christ Conquers), were chanted at solemn crown-wearings, when the king's majesty was projected through visual symbolism.[21] The long obituary on William I which occurs in the E-text of the *Anglo-Saxon Chronicle* includes the following passage:

> He was very dignified. He wore his crown three times every year, whenever he was in England. At Easter he wore it at Winchester, at Whitsuntide at Westminster, and at Christmas at Gloucester. On those occasions all the powerful men from all over England were with him: archbishops, bishops, abbots and earls, thegns and knights.[22]

A similar statement occurs in William of Malmesbury's Latin *Life* of St. Wulfstan, who was bishop of Worcester

---

20 M. McCormick, *Eternal Victory: triumphal rulership in late antiquity, Byzantium and the early medieval West*, (2nd ed., Cambridge, 1990), 78-9, 184-5, 188, 258-9, 384-7.

21 W.L. Warren, *The Governance of Norman and Angevin England 1086-1272*, (London, 1987), 17.

22 *The Anglo-Saxon Chronicle*, ed. and transl. Dorothy Whitelock, with D.C. Douglas and Susie I. Tucker (London, 1961) 164.

from 1062 to 1095. The reader is told that:

> King William had brought in a custom which
> his successors followed for a while and then
> allowed to lapse: this was that three times a
> year all the magnates met together at his court,
> to discuss the essential business of the realm,
> and at the same time behold the king in his
> glory, wearing his crown set with precious
> stones.[23]

A seasonal crown-wearing served as a forum in which
matters of political consequence were debated by the
king and the powerful men of the realm. Since the magnates commanded the manpower which could thwart the
king's intentions, a consensus was established whenever
possible. The solemn crown-wearing conveyed a visible
reminder to the barons that the king claimed to assert an
authority which was on a higher level than their own,
and the spectacular ceremony was designed to prompt
acquiescence in his policies, however uncongenial. The
writer of William I's obituary notice in the *Anglo-Saxon
Chronicle* made the connection between the impressive
ritual and the extent of the king's powers:

> He was a very stern and violent man, so that
> no-one dared do anything contrary to his will.
> Earls who acted against his will were put in
> chains. He expelled bishops from their sees,
> and abbots from their abbacies, and put thegns

---

23 *The Vita Wulfstani of William of Malmesbury*, ed. R.R. Darlington,
Camden Third series, 40, (1928), 34.

in prison, and finally . . . his own brother . . .
Odo.[24]

The visible majesty of the crowned king, the *christus domini*, the Lord's Anointed, was reminiscent of the image of Christ as Judge, which recurred in sculpture or murals in churches throughout the land. The Domesday Survey which was made on the orders of the king and revealed to him the resources of his realm, was so called by contemporaries, who equated it with the revelations of the Last Judgement.[25]

William of Malmesbury post-dates the introduction of the ceremony, since there is some evidence of crown-wearings in late Anglo-Saxon England.[26] In the reign of Edward the Confessor those locations which later became the traditional ones began to be used on a regular basis. He relinquished London for Westminster, with its new palace, but he also made occasional use of the rural palace of Windsor.[27] The ceremonial followed much the same pattern in the reigns of William I and his sons. The crown would be placed on the king's head in his palace before he went in public procession to the church. The

---

24 *Anglo-Saxon Chronicle*, ed. Whitelock et al., 164.

25 Nelson, *Politics and Ritual in early medieval Europe*, 400.

26 Warren, *The Governance of Norman and Angevin England*, 17.

27 M. Biddle, 'Seasonal Festivals and Residence: Winchester, Westminster and Gloucester in the tenth to twelfth Centuries', *Anglo-Norman Studies VIII. Proceedings of the Battle Conference 1985*, ed. R. Allen Brown (Woodbridge, 1986), 59, 69.

greater Anglo-Saxon churches had a west-work, with a balcony, on which the crowned king probably made a formal appearance to the crowds gathered outside, before he processed back to his palace.[28] In this way, the local populace was given the opportunity to be impressed by the manifestation of royal majesty. But for political purposes it was necessary to convey this visual imagery to the great men of the realm, so that a large palace was as essential as a big church when deciding where to hold a crown-wearing. Edward's move, from the cramped old residence in the city of London to his new palace beside his rebuilt minster to the west of the city, should be understood in this light,[29] as must the rebuilding of this palace of Westminster by William Rufus, and his reported criticism that even his own new Westminster Hall was not nearly big enough.[30] Ostentation had a serious political purpose. The royal residence at Gloucester was not expanded, and this location fell out of use. Windsor, used occasionally by William I, gradually became a regular substitute in the reigns of his sons, but Henry I allowed crown-wearings to lapse on any regular basis.[31] Throughout the twelfth century - and indeed for several centuries more, court ritual played an important role in

---

28 *Ibid.*, 59.

29 Gervase Rosser, *Medieval Westminster 1200-1540*, (Oxford, 1989), 14.

30 Henry of Huntingdon, *The History of the English*, ed. T. Arnold, Rolls Series, (London, 1879), 231.

31 Biddle, 'Seasonal Festivals and Residence', 51-63, esp. 52, 59.

underlining political concepts.[32] Crown-wearings did not suddenly become anachronistic. It was rather that Henry ensured stability by keeping a close watch over his English subjects.[33] He also came under the puritanical influence of Robert de Beaumont, who urged a policy of retrenchment.[34]

The bigger churches were also used in another ceremony which manifested the majesty of the king. A passage in the so-called 'First Charter of William I' for Westminster abbey - one of the more spectacular forgeries produced there - runs:

> And whenever I return from any military expedition, whether from Normandy or [elsewhere] beyond the frontiers of England, and I visit Westminster abbey . . . and I am received with glory and honour by the monks in procession, I have vowed a mark of gold, according to the pious institution of this custom by my predecessors.[35]

Westminster, inspired by its contacts with the French

---

32 D.A. Bullough, 'Games People Played: Drama and Ritual as Propaganda in Medieval Europe', *Transactions of the Royal Historical Society*, fifth series, 24, (1974), 97-112.

33 *English Historical Documents 1042-1189*, 320.

34 J.O. Prestwich, 'The Military Household of the Norman kings', *English Historical Review*, 96, (1981), 29-30.

35 *Calendar of the Charter Rolls*, IV, 1327-1341, 335.

12

royal abbey of St. Denis,[36] was claiming to be the traditional setting for a 'joyful entry' of the kind practised by
Continental rulers, including, it seems, William himself
in his capacity as duke of Normandy.[37] The reference to
the king's predecessors suggests that the ritual was used
by Edward the Confessor. He perhaps experienced such
solemnities during his exile on the Continent, when he
was accorded royal rank,[38] and may have been a privileged spectator at such ceremonies. Solemn receptions
were certainly given to the Norman kings by the greater
religious houses, and Archbishop Lanfranc, in his *Monastic Constitutions*, outlined the role which his monks
of Christchurch, Canterbury, were to play on those occasions.[39] At the end of the twelfth century, both Richard I
and his brother King John, when returning to England
from overseas, made solemn visits to certain abbeys.
These comprised Canterbury (the mother-church of Chris-
tianity in England); St. Albans (the shrine of the English
proto-martyr) and Bury St. Edmunds (the shrine of an

---

36 Antonia Gransden, 'Baldwin, abbot of Bury St. Edmunds, 1065-
1097', *Proceedings of the Battle Conference on Anglo-Norman Studies
IV 1981*, ed. R. Allen Brown (Woodbridge, 1982), 68-71; B.W.
Scholz, 'Two forged charters from the abbey of Westminster and
their relationship with St Denis', *English Historical Review*, 76
(1961), 466-7.

37 Nelson, *Politics and Ritual in early medieval Europe*, 396.

38 Simon Keynes, 'The Athelings in Exile in Normandy', *Anglo-
Norman Studies XIII Proceedings of the Battle Conference 1990*,
ed. Marjorie Chibnall (Woodbridge, 1991). 185, 190-1, 193-4, 196-
200.

39 *Decreta Lanfranci*, 70-2, 74.

East Anglian king 'martyred' by pagan Danes).[40]

III

The role of churchmen in the royal rituals was potentially double-edged. The prelates who assisted at royal rituals hoped that these would impress not only the congregation, but also the king himself, and that he would realise the tremendous responsibility he undertook in receiving the power to represent the will of God on earth.[41] The Norman kings, like their English predecessors, promised at their coronation that the church of God and the whole Christian people within their dominions would keep true peace; that they would forbid anyone from pillaging or doing harm to men of any social class; and that they would insist on justice and mercy being observed in all legal verdicts, in order that God in return would be merciful to the king and his subjects.[42] Churchmen recognized the need for a strong royal authority, to protect them against rapacious magnates, but they did not want to be subject to someone who domineered over them. They argued that the king's unction did not confer on him powers over the clergy, and reminded him that his anointing was bestowed only after he had solemnly promised to protect the Church and its ministers, and to

---

40 Emma Mason, 'St. Wulfstan's Staff: A Legend and its Uses', *Medium Aevum*, 53 (1984), 157 and note 7.

41 Warren, *The Governance of Norman and Angevin England*, 16.

42 Frank Barlow, *Edward the Confessor*, (London, 1970), 63.

respect the laws of the realm.[43]

Royal authority was best upheld in a peaceful, law-abiding realm, and the well-being of the Church was believed to be conducive towards the stability of royal rule.[44] But when it came to the administration of justice, the Norman kings lacked the resources to deal directly with much of the wrongdoing committed by and against the majority of their poorer subjects. Their attention was chiefly given to pleas brought by the more affluent ecclesiastics and laymen who were prepared to pay heavily for a favourable royal verdict. The hierarchy of lesser courts, whether of barony, shire, hundred or manor, dealt with most of the lawsuits of the lesser people.

While clerical theorists tried to harness royal power, they also added a dimension to its validity. A new element introduced into the coronation ceremony by William the Conqueror was the adoption of the French practice of asking the congregation whether it was their wish that he should be crowned as their lord.[45] The experimental question was retained in subsequent coronations, and the required answer reinforced the king's authority. To help render this verdict a nation-wide one, the king was mentioned by name and title at every recital of Mass - both

---

43 Warren, *The Governance of Norman and Angevin England*, 16.

44 Emma Mason, '*Pro statu et incolumnitate regni mei:* royal monastic patronage, 1066-1154', in *Religion and National Identity*, ed. S. Mews, Studies in Church History, 18 (Oxford, 1982), 99-117.

45 M.T. Clanchy, *England and its Rulers 1066-1272: foreign lordship and national identity* (London, 1983), 44.

in England and in Normandy.[46] The validity of his rule was hammered home on every possible public occasion, and resistance to the anointed king was deemed a sin.

During the reigns of the Norman kings, writers on kingship drew on the concept of Christian kingship which had been devised in late ninth-century Francia, for the heirs of Charlemagne. It was maintained that the Christian king received, through his unction, Divine grace which conferred upon him the right to rule, and set him above other laymen. The king exercized delegated Divine power, and his subjects owed him the obedience due to the man chosen by God to exercize rule on earth. They described the ideal king as brave, prudent, self-restrained, an upholder of justice, wise, merciful and God-fearing.[47]

But the claims of the reformed and reforming papacy mitigated the efforts of royal propagandists in the later eleventh century and the earlier twelfth. While many senior churchmen were content to co-operate with the secular power, there were others in successive generations who took a stand in support of ecclesiastical rights which threatened to weaken the royal position, as in the case of Archbishop Anselm in the reign of William Rufus and more especially in the early years of Henry I.[48] In the

---

46 Hollister, *Monarchy, Magnates and Institutions*, 21.

47 Warren, *The Governance of Norman and Angevin England*, 15-16.

48 Frank Barlow, *The English Church 1066-1154* (London, 1979), 287-92, 297-302.

reign of Stephen, the weakening of royal power enabled Archbishop Theobald and other churchmen to widen their own jurisdiction and, in doing so, to undermine the king's authority even more.[49]

Throughout the reigns of the Norman kings, there were clerics who held a wide range of views on the extent and limitations of the royal powers. Even those who were on the whole favourable to the royal claims, and appreciated the good order which resulted from strong rule, maintained that the interests of the clerical hierarchy should also be upheld. Others argued that the king was bound to observe a contractual relationship with his subjects. If he demanded their support, then they were entitled to considerate government. One anonymous writer compiled several conflicting views and cited the arguments which could be used in each, but made no attempt to draw conclusions.[50] While members of the clerical hierarchy occasionally tried to place restrictions on royal action, and kings for their part preferred to see such assertive clerics as Archbishops Anselm and Theobald in exile, there was, on the whole, a realization that the king needed his clerics, to uphold his authority, just as they needed him to guarantee them their lands and privileges in the face of baronial aggression.

There is anecdotal evidence that kings regarded the powerful spiritual services of the clergy as a commodity which could be bought. Dissident churchmen, however eminent, received brusque treatment. Any bishop, in his

---

49 *Ibid*, 302-10.

50 Warren, *The Governance of Norman and Angevin England*, 18.

spiritual capacity, could heap ecclesiastical penalties upon laymen yet in a crisis such as that involving William of St. Calais, bishop of Durham, or, for instance, those involving Archbishops Anselm and Theobald, the kings and their advisors regarded these clerics as having two distinct identities. To treat a bishop harshly, on political grounds, was not to reject the doctrines of the church - but rather to check the continuing encroachment of the ecclesiastical power on the sphere of secular jurisdiction. Pope Gregory VII (1073-85) and his supporters might argue that their reforms were simply a conservative return to 'right order' but lay rulers regarded such developments as revolutionary.[51] In the wake of the papal reform, it was at first still possible for a ruler to rid himself of a troublesome or inconvenient cleric provided that papal approval was obtained at all stages. William the Conqueror contrived the deposition of Archbishop Stigand in 1070, but increasingly any effort to remove or even thwart a prelate without papal agreement provoked a sharp response. This created political difficulties - as with Archbishop Anselm in the reigns of William Rufus and Henry I, or with Bishop Roger of Salisbury and his kinsmen, in 1139.

The increasingly vocal assertion of its rights by the spiritual hierarchy, and in particular the spread of papal claims through the use of legates and a developing judicial system, posed a challenge to the sovereignty of the Norman rulers. The rebirth of legal studies throughout Western Europe helped to meet this challenge, and secular law concerning the rights of kings became more explicit.

---

51 Barlow, *The English Church 1066-1154*, 271-5.

Even so a head-on clash with the spiritual hierarchy became steadily more impractical. Royal interests were furthered by lobbying at the papal court, or by negotiating with visiting papal legates, although those astute diplomats sometimes proved more than a match - as in the attempt by William Rufus to secure the removal of Archbishop Anselm.[52]

On another level the institutions of the church could be utilized to serve the interests of the monarchy. Contemporaries expected that kings would be generous patrons of the church, whether by founding new religious houses or by making substantial gifts, or concessions of rights and privileges, to existing religious houses, but many charters relating to such gifts and concessions are worded so as to blur over the fact that some substantial financial recompense was required by the royal donor. The interests of the Norman kings were best served if the appearance of generosity could be sustained at minimal cost - a practice in which they followed their pre-Conquest predecessors - donating land which had only recently been acquired - usually through forfeiture.[53] Religious houses themselves also petitioned the king for exemption from various financial exactions which were routinely due to the crown. Clerical petitioners paid heavily for grants of exemptions, which depleted the royal revenues only to a small extent, but could make a big difference to the

---

52 *Ibid.*, 291.

53 *Westminster Abbey Charters 1066-c.1214*, ed. Emma Mason, assisted by the late Jennifer Bray, continuing the work of the late Desmond J. Murphy (London Record Society, 25, 1988), nos. 6, 10, 16-18.

annual income of a monastery.

Royal patronage was granted to a few privileged religious houses on a much more substantial basis, because their churches were intended to be the mausolea of particular kings, located at the hub of their realm and serving as a focus for political loyalty, a concept which had ancient antecedents in England. William the Conqueror and Queen Matilda were buried in the religious houses which they had respectively founded in Caen, which they perceived as the hub of their territories. The patronage which William Rufus bestowed on Gloucester abbey perhaps originated in his intention that this should become his mausoleum. But his death in the New Forest, and the urgency with which his brother Henry needed to complete antecedent formalities before his own consecration, caused William Rufus to be buried at Winchester, the mausoleum of the kings of the house of Wessex, and of Cnut and Harthacnut. Both Henry I and Stephen founded and endowed religious houses which they designated as their mausolea - respectively Reading and Faversham.

Each Norman king also granted benefactions 'for the stability and security of my realm', both to royal mausolea and also to other favoured monasteries. In his charter of donation, the king voiced his expectation that the monks would pray for his physical and spiritual well-being, and that consequently his gift would be recompensed by political stability.[54] Various considerations might prompt the wording of charters in this way, but usually

---

54 Mason, 'Pro statu et incolumnitate regni mei', 99-117.

there was some particular reason, as in the case of Westminster abbey. William the Conqueror, who claimed to be the lawful successor of Edward the Confessor, found it expedient to be crowned in the latter's church of Westminster, as Harold Godwinson had done earlier. William's sons and their own successors followed suit, establishing Westminster as the unchallenged coronation church, although before the time of Henry III no post-Conquest king regarded the abbey as his mausoleum or as a unique focus for the royal cult. The only special attention which Westminster received was in a brief period during the succession crisis caused by the death of Henry I's only legitimate son, in November 1120.[55]

IV

Crises recurred during the Anglo-Norman period. The endemic restiveness of the king's subjects was contained by combining the assertion of his theoretical sovereignty with stringent practical measures. The Norman triumph at Hastings could be regarded as the victory of the rightful candidate in the latest of an ongoing series of succession disputes - a viewpoint which helped surviving Englishmen of any consequence to rationalize the submission which they had initially made on grounds of common prudence.[56] The dispossession of the great English secular magnates, and their replacement by the followers

---

55 Emma Mason, 'Westminster abbey and the monarchy between the reigns of William I and John (1066-1216), *Journal of Ecclesiastical History*, 41 (1990), 199-216.

56 Stafford, *Unification and Conquest*, 102.

of William the Conqueror, removed one potential cause of political stability only to create another. In the decades before the Norman Conquest, the English nobles had unhesitatingly furthered their ambitions by violent means, calling on help from beyond the frontiers. The more restive French among their territorial successors asserted their own power by the same means. French-speakers led the resistance to royal authority while the English, more accustomed to strong royal rule, supported the Norman king who was their only guarantor of stability.[57] But the oppressiveness of later Anglo-Saxon royal rule was echoed in the harsh exactions of William the Conqueror. By virtue of his coronation he could claim the rights and authority of an English king although his victory enabled him to rule more harshly and with less restraint than a native-born king might have done.

The underlying purpose of the Domesday Survey was to ascertain the full extent of his title to rights and lands, in all but the barely governable northernmost parts of England, and to check on the activities of his sheriffs.[58] The conquest and the ensuing confiscations gave William I command of a greatly extended royal demesne, but this continued to fluctuate in extent, as it had done formerly. It was gradually eroded again by the need of William Rufus and Henry I to make grants to influential magnates.[59] Such grants alleviated the tensions which arose from a conflict between the ever-more effective royal

---

57 *Ibid.*, 103, 105.

58 *Ibid.*, 106-8.

59 *Ibid*, 112.

administration, with its growing capacity to impose financial and military demands on the population, and on the other hand, the entrenched rights of mighty subjects. Chroniclers accused the Norman kings of avarice, but similar allegations were made about their royal predecessors, at least from the time of Ethelred II.[60]

The Norman kings were not only royal sovereigns, like their English predecessors, but also feudal lords, a role which enabled them to subject baronial restiveness to constraint. The king, from his vantage-point at the peak of the feudal pyramid, was in a position to reinforce his own powers; reward loyal supporters or demote dissidents by manipulation of the patronage which accrued to him under feudal custom. But feudal custom and obligations were not allowed to operate to the detriment of the rights of the sovereign. The Salisbury Oath, exacted in August 1086, established the principle that all the king's subjects had obligations to him which overrode those they owed to any intermediate feudal lord, and this gave the king direct control over the military potential of the realm. The royal sovereignty was also asserted by interventions to control the economic potential of the kingdom: by ordering officials to protect travelling merchants and traders; legislating on conditions of sales; and providing an acceptable medium of exchange in a uniform coinage of a reliable quality.[61] But whenever the king's assertion of his sovereignty was disputed, he asserted the

---

60 Robin Frame, *The Political Development of the British Isles 1100-1400* (Oxford, 1990), 81.

61 Warren, *The Governance of Norman and Angevin England*, 20-21.

prerogatives inherent in feudal overlordship. Successful
kingship depended upon knowing when to move from
one mode of action to the other.[62]

Royal policies, and indeed royal authority, were justified
by appealing to the past. William the Conqueror strength-
ened his authority by claiming to be the kinsman of
Edward the Confessor, and that consequently he ruled
over the realm by hereditary right.[63] Later Norman kings
made the same point in their charters by reference to
their kinship with their immediate predecessors: 'my father', 'my brother', 'my uncle', or 'my kinsman'. But
while the authority of the reigning king was reinforced
by appeal to hereditary right, primogeniture did not appeal to candidates for the crown. William II, Henry I and
Stephen were all younger sons. Each had an elder brother
living at the time he became king of England. The existence of bye-passed siblings, and other ambitious kindred,
contributed to the underlying instability of Norman rule.
To survive, each king needed exceptional ability and
strength of character, coupled with the loyal service of
astute ministers.[64] A successful Norman king was not
simply an ambitious war-leader, with clearly defined political goals. He also needed to establish and maintain a
complex network of diplomatic arrangements if his military victories were to have any long-term impact. The
ruler had to be tenacious of his overall objectives, and
aware of what could be achieved by bribery and political

---

62 Erickson, *The Medieval Vision*, 117-118.

63 Clanchy, *England and its Rulers*, 43.

64 *Ibid.*, 66-7.

intrigue, even though the minutiae of diplomacy, with its concomitant bribery and intriguing, were left to his subordinates. Unflagging energy and persistence contributed to the success of William the Conqueror and his two successors, just as the lack of these qualities contributed to the failure of William's eldest son, Robert Curthose, and latterly, also, that of Stephen.[65]

The personal abilities of the ruler were all-important in an era when the government was still largely focused on the king's household, and changes in policy resulted from the words he uttered. The routine of administration was entrusted to clerks - the ablest of whom were in due course entrusted with the lands and liberties of a bishopric, but overall policy was determined by the king himself - perhaps influenced by those he chose to consult on the point in question. These advisors varied considerably. 'New men' - trained clerks and ambitious men from lesser landed families - largely conducted the administration, particularly with regard to finance. Some, such as Ranulf Flambard, were reputed to have inaugurated unpopular policies, but while long-serving royal clerks might influence the course of royal policy, certain privileged magnates also did so.[66]

V

The ambitions of the Norman kings, and the constraints under which they acted, ensured that the royal lifestyle

---

65 Erickson, *The Medieval Vision*, 140.

66 *Ibid.*, 121.

was continuously stressful. These kings were engaged in almost constant travel, often with some crisis facing them at the end of their journey. When diplomatic initiatives failed, they must be prepared to fight, and it was essential for any medieval ruler that he should be a successful war-leader. Political achievements were at best the outcome of averting one crisis or another and such short-lived peace as there was, most often concluded with wars or with rumours of wars. It was this endemic instability which earned the Norman kings their grasping reputation, since they had a constant need of money, both to hire mercenary troops and to provide bribes for potential allies. Complaints about the searching enquiries of the Domesday commissioners, or about the royal exploitation of the 'feudal incidents' - the occasional windfalls which accrued to the king as head of the feudal pyramid - must be seen against a background of constant financial pressure as the kings tried to defend their extended frontiers, both of England and of their Continental lands.[67]

Instability on the frontiers - and baronial rebellion - were not the only sources of stress with which the Norman kings contended. Heavy taxation prompted endemic resentment. Grimbald, the physician of Henry I, reported that the king was tormented by nightmares of irate clerics, knights and peasants.[68] This incident highlights the fact that while the Norman kings generally acted in an autocratic and aggressive fashion, asserting their own rights at the expense of others, yet the effectiveness of

---

67 Ibid., 123, 127.

68 Zarnecki, Holt and Holland (eds.), *English Romanesque Art*, 102-3, no. 33.

their rule was variable - and ultimately dependent on the judgement of discontented subjects as to whether the king could retaliate decisively if they took matters into their own hands.[69] Awareness of this precarious situation was not conducive to the royal peace of mind, and yet the whole edifice of royal rule depended upon the self-confidence of the ruler and his own belief in his success.

Dangers lurked within the court itself, where courtiers competed for the limited amount of patronage which was available at any given time.[70] Courtiers were notoriously jealous of one another and resentful when some rival was promoted over their heads. Pent-up resentment might provoke an aggrieved royal servant into an attack upon the king - as the ultimate cause of his own frustration.[71] There is a strong probability that William Rufus was assassinated - most likely at the instigation of Prince Louis of France.[72] Henry I is said to have evaded an assassination attempt by Herbert the chamberlain, and gone in fear of further attacks.[73] Members of the royal

---

69 Erickson, *The Medieval Vision*, 125.

70 J.E. Lally, 'Secular Patronage at the court of King Henry II', *Bulletin of the Institute of Historical Research*, 49 (1976), 168-9; Walter Map, *De Nugis Curialium: A Courtier's Trifles*, ed. and transl. M.R. James, rev. C.N.L. Brooke and R.A.B. Mynors (Oxford, 1983), 13-17, 373.

71 Erickson, *The Medieval Vision*, 125, 128.

72 Emma Mason, 'William Rufus and the Historians', *Medieval History* 1:1 (1991), 18-20.

73 *English Historical Documents, 1042-1189*, 321; Hollister, *Monarchy, Magnates and Institutions*, 214.

household could easily approach the king without arous-
ing suspicion, and aggrieved courtiers might well be open
to bribes by discontented barons, or by the agents of
foreign powers. To combat such risks, as well as to
assist their military plans, eleventh and twelfth century
governments deployed a secret intelligence network just
as their predecessors had done in earlier reigns.[74]

Reliable intelligence was essential to the Norman kings
of England, given the extent of the lands which they
governed, and the constant threats to their various frontiers. The decision by William I to create a multi-na-
tional realm by seizing England, in addition to govern-
ing Normandy and Maine, created a new range of problems for himself and successive kings of the English.
Although King Edgar, in the tenth century, claimed recognition as overlord of the other peoples of Britain, little
was done to implement this claim. In the reign of Edward the Confessor, campaigns were launched against
the Welsh by Harold and Tostig Godwinson and, with
less success, by Edward's nephew Ralph, the earl of
Hereford, but the English advance was limited.[75] Under
the Normans there was a series of sustained drives into
Wales. A vigorous advance against the Scots, in the
reigns of William the Conqueror and William Rufus,
secured Norman control as far north as the Tweed-Solway

---

74 Jean Deuve, *Les Services Secrets normands: La Guerre Secrete
au Moyen Age (900-1135)*, (Conde-sur-Noireau, 1990).

75 K.L. Maund, 'The Welsh Alliances of Earl Alfgar of Mercia and
his family in the mid-eleventh century', *Anglo-Norman Studies XI.
proceedings of the Battle Conference 1988*, ed. R. Allen Brown
(Woodbridge, 1989), 181-90.

frontier.[76] These additional territories within Britain presented enough problems for the effective assertion of royal authority, but there were further difficulties caused by ongoing tensions on the Continent, resulting from the determination of the Norman kings to secure and reinforce their territories of Normandy and Maine. This determination inevitably gave rise to conflict with the king of France, and with the great nobles of the region.[77]

VI

The Norman kings of England were also vassals of the King of France, in their capacity as dukes of Normandy, but in practice they barely admitted this. William the Conqueror, as duke of Normandy, rendered homage to King Philip I of France in 1060, but never did so after becoming king of England. William Rufus never rendered homage as king, nor did Henry I, although, when Louis VI of France threatened to support Robert Curthose's son, William Clito, against him, Henry allowed his own son, William Atheling, to render homage. King Stephen negotiated a similar compromise through his son Eustace.[78]

The Norman kings effectively ruled England, Normandy

---

76 W.E. Kapelle, *The Norman Conquest of the North: the Region and its Transformation 1000-1135*, (London, 1979), 120-57.

77 J. Le Patourel, *The Norman Empire* (Oxford, 1976), 73-88; Hollister, *Monarchy, Magnates and Institutions*, 17-57.

78 Hollister, *Monarchy, Magnates and Institutions*, 41-2, 49.

and Maine as one political unit. It is doubtful whether William the Conqueror expected that William Rufus would eventually succeed to his whole cross-Channel realm, but he was determined to do so. Consequently William Rufus held the Anglo-Norman realm in its entirety between 1096 and 1100, after Normandy was mortgaged to him by Robert Curthose in order to finance his crusade. Robert held the Continental patrimony again only from 1100 to 1106. It was then won from him by Henry I, whose Continental lands were effectively transmitted to Stephen, together with the English throne, in December 1135, but were lost to Geoffrey of Anjou in the early 1140s.

England and Normandy were therefore two components of one realm for most of the time between late 1066 and 1140, and at the outset of this period the greatest magnates held lands on both sides of the Channel, while Norman religious houses were granted lands in England.[79] But over the ensuing generations there was a shift in this balance. Great families, with some exceptions, divided their Continental and English lands so that one son inherited each. Some great families lost their English lands altogether, and 'new men' profited by grants made from these forfeitures. Where rising curial families can be traced back to their Continental origins, it is often found to be the case that they held little land there - so that their rise to fame and fortune was experienced largely in an English context.[80] Similarly, the great wave of new

79 *Ibid.*, 23-4, 28.

80 Emma Mason, 'Magnates, Curiales and the Wheel of Fortune', *Proceedings of the Battle Conference on Anglo-Norman Studies II. 1979*, ed. R. Allen Brown (Woodbridge, 1980), 131-6.

religious houses founded in England after about 1100 were English in their orientation. Like the older English abbeys, they were normally given Norman heads, but these men quickly fostered the cults of old English saints, as the guarantors of their rights.[81]

England and Normandy had separate judicial systems, but were held together by the itinerant royal court, headed by the person of the king. The two components of the Anglo-Norman realm were not administered in an identical fashion although their administrations displayed marked parallels. The church hierarchies remained distinct, but ambitious careerists were promoted from one side of the Channel to the other. The financial systems also remained distinct, with separate treasuries at Rouen and Winchester, although English bullion crossed the Channel to finance the kings' Continental projects. Treasury officials from England are occasionally recorded in Normandy and some were drowned in the wreck of the White Ship in November 1120.[82] But conquered England was kept on a tighter reign than Normandy. English feudal quotas were higher than those required in Normandy, and English sheriffs were less independent than Norman vicomtes.[83] It was the personal will of the kings which kept the two components of their realm from fall-

81 Susan J. Ridyard, '*Condigna Veneratio*: Post-Conquest Attitudes to the Saints of the Anglo-Saxons', *Anglo-Norman Studies IX. Proceedings of the Battle Conference 1986*, ed. R. Allen Brown (Woodbridge, 1987), 179-206.

82 *The Ecclesiastical History of Orderic Vitalis*, VI, ed. Marjorie Chibnall (Oxford, 1978), 304-5.

83 Hollister, *Monarchy, Magnates and Institutions*, 15, 25.

ing apart. In Normandy they were legally only dukes yet they governed the duchy as king, using that style in their writs.[84]

VII

The person of the king was the hub around which government revolved, so that arrangements were made for a deputed authority during his absence from either component of his realm. Long-standing tradition prescribed that a ruler should appoint close members of his family as subordinate rulers. William the Conqueror relied on his wife Matilda, with two close advisors, the magnate Roger de Beaumont and John, archbishop of Rouen, to represent him in Normandy, while in England the king's half-brother Odo, bishop of Bayeux and earl of Kent, exercized delegated authority for much of the reign, in association with William Fitz Osbern (in the early years) and Archbishop Lanfranc. The role of the great churchmen was in line with earlier practice, not only in Normandy but also in England, where clerics such as Archbishops Dunstan or Stigand had played a part in government. Arrangements of this kind were modified in the reign of William Rufus, who lacked a wife and was repeatedly in dispute with his brothers. In this reign, another cleric, Ranulf Flambard, came into greater prominence, being rewarded latterly with the bishopric of Durham. His control over the financial administration was supported by a team of experienced curial officers. Henry I resumed the practice of delegating authority: first, to his wife, Queen

---

84 *Ibid.*, 30.

Edith Matilda, and after her death in 1118, to their son
William Atheling, who died in November 1120. In addition, Archbishop Anselm, in his last years, perhaps oc-
cupied the political role which Lanfranc exercized earlier. This reign also saw the renewed appointment of a
chief financial officer - in this case Roger, bishop of
Salisbury, who continued in post down to June 1139,
latterly supported by younger kinsmen in subordinate
offices.[85] Henry I's second wife, Alice, seems not to have
exercized delegated authority on the same scale as her
predecessor, but in the crisis of 1141 it was Stephen's
wife, yet another Matilda, who saved the day for his
cause against the forces of her cousin, the Empress Matilda.

The political role of the queen-consort could be crucial,
as shown in this instance. Another duty of the queen-
consort was to breed legitimate male heirs for her hus-
band, and it was advantageous if she transmitted the
genes of earlier rulers.[86] But the day-to-day influence of
the queen-consort was exercized through the medium of
the royal household. She might well have a voice in the
distribution of patronage, and might mediate on behalf
of those important men who had earned the royal dis-
pleasure. By doing so, she affected the conduct of politics. It was certainly her role to supervise the royal household in such a way that visitors were impressed by the

---

85 David Bates, 'The Origins of the Justiciarship', *Proceedings of
the Battle Conference on Anglo-Norman Studies. IV. 1981*, ed. R.
Allen Brown (Woodbridge, 1982), 1-12.

86 Christopher Brooke, *The Saxon and Norman Kings*, (2nd ed.,
1967), 151, 170, 181.

magnificent style in which the ruler lived - one important expression of his political power.

But the queen-consort also established the public image of the court. Her high birth, and her position as the lawful and consecrated wife of the king, and the mother of his heir, guaranteed her right to dictate the public conduct of the courtiers, and hence determine the reputation of the king's court. The unseemly activities of the courtiers of William Rufus, of which Archbishop Anselm complained so strongly, would never have been allowed to persist, and thereby cause scandal, if the king had been lawfully married to a wife authorized to establish the tone of his court.[87] The Welsh chronicler blamed the king's reliance on mistresses for his lack of a lawful heir.[88] But these women also lacked the authority to curb the disreputable activities of the courtiers, which in turn caused William Rufus himself to earn a hostile reputation in the Anglo-Norman chronicles. There was always a potential risk of wild doings at the royal court, frequented as it was both by rich people with the leisure for self-indulgence, and also by large numbers of footloose warriors.

---

87 Elizabeth Ward, 'Caesar's Wife: The Career of the Empress Judith, 819-29', in *Charlemagne's Heir: New Perspectives on the reign of Louis the Pious (814-840)*, ed. P. Godman and R. Collins (Oxford, 1990), 205-27. I am grateful to Ms. Ward for a discussion on the relevance of her findings to the court of the Norman Kings, and in particular to that of William Rufus.

88 *Brut y Tywysogion or The Chronicle of the Princes*, ed. T. Jones (Cardiff, 1955), 41.

The successful campaigns of the Norman kings owed much to their military household, the *familia regis*. The concept of an elite military force, ready to go into action at any time, can be traced in England from the time of King Alfred onwards, and is clearly perceived in the housecarls of King Cnut. The chronicler Orderic Vitalis reported on some of the activities of the military household of William the Conqueror, and, in far more detail, on those of William Rufus and Henry I. The household was very mixed in its social composition, comprising feudal vassals; men retained by annual money-fiefs; mercenaries, and those serving for hope of future reward - whether in the form of new grants of land or that of the restitution of forfeited estates.[89] Members of this household served as leaders of the king's fighting force, but they might also be entrusted with administrative responsibilities, including the defence of key shires.[90] The members of the *familia* were drawn from Brittany, Flanders and France as well as from Normandy. They were loyal over and above the hope of tangible reward, proud to serve a king who had the reputation of being a magnificent war-leader, and generous patron of his fighting force, hence the ability of William Rufus to attract so powerful a following, despite the fact that he did not commit his troops to any major battle. The Norman kings offered rewards and promises to deter potential recruits from going elsewhere, whether to join the victorious Normans

---

89 Prestwich, 'The Military Household of the Norman Kings', 6, 10, 13; Marjorie Chibnall, 'Mercenaries and the Familia Regis under Henry I', *History*, 62 (1977), 15-23.

90 Prestwich, 'The Military Household of the Norman Kings', 22-3.

of Sicily or South Italy, or on the Crusade.[91] The *familia regis* played an important role throughout the reigns of the Norman kings, including that of Stephen, when it was led by William of Ypres.[92] But the *familia regis* was criticized because of its habit of consuming all that lay in its path - in the manner of a troop of looting conquerors rather than of the king's own army, hence the regulations imposed by Henry I in order to discipline its activities.[93] His rulings may have taken effect for a while, but the seemingly insatiable appetite of the royal forces, and their reluctance to pay for what they took, recurred as a contentious issue throughout the thirteenth century and beyond.[94]

Criticism, not simply of the *familia regis*, but also of other agents of royal authority, permeates the major chronicles of the period. One reason for this is that, in general, the monasteries were subjected to a far greater range of royal exactions in the generations after the Conquest than had been the case earlier, so that monastic writers took to voicing the grievances of all the oppressed in a way in which their predecessors would not have done.[95] A major reason for the hated royal exactions was that the

---

91 *Ibid.*, 26-8.

92 *Ibid.*, 35.

93 *Ibid.*, 29. See also *English Historical Documents 1042-1189*, 320, no. 8 (c).

94 *English Historical Documents 1189-1327*, ed. Harry Rothwell (London, 1975), nos. 80, 99, 124-6.

95 Stafford, *Unification and Conquest*, 106.

kings were threatened by the turmoil which always lay just under the surface, whether in the form of rumoured Scandinavian invasions in the reign of William the Conqueror - or the unrest which intermittently threatened his three successors. Even when England itself was calm, there was a constant fear for the safety of the Continental component of their realm. Ensuring the safety of Normandy placed an enormous financial burden on England. Exactions had to be stepped up - so causing further resentment. Much depended on the loyalty and acumen of the king's financial experts, since by controlling the revenues they enabled the king to maintain the troops who could quell the rebels.[96] It was a cyclic movement, since the more money that was extorted, the more criticism of royal rule. Royal government was inevitably repressive, with an underlying threat of violence against the individual as well as against rebel forces.[97]

The dominant, and necessarily domineering, role of the king is reflected in the language of royal administration - 'my barons, my courts, my sheriff'. The missives which deployed this language were drafted by his advisors, in the face of potential baronial dissension and aspirant separatism. These royal advisors were increasingly recruited from those with some knowledge, not only of canon law, but also of the civil law which had guaranteed the autocratic rule of the Roman emperors. Men with some knowledge of 'the two laws' could therefore define and rationalize the king's authority, and project it

---

96 Clanchy, *England and its Rulers*, 75-6.

97 Hollister, *Monarchy, Magnates and Institutions*, 291-301.

in the peremptory language of the royal writs.[98]

Criticism of authoritarian royal rule frequently focused on the harsh maintenance of the royal forests, as though these were some novelty introduced at the arbitrary whim of the Norman kings. In fact both King Cnut and Edward the Confessor maintained royal forests, although after 1066 the New Forest and others were safeguarded with an unprecedented degree of severity. The forests were exclusive royal hunting preserves and recreational areas, their publicly-acknowledged reason for existence.[99] But additionally they could give the king the pre-emptive control over land - the most valuable resource of a period when the population was steadily rising. From the Pipe Rolls of the Angevin period, it is clear that forest land was treated as a source of revenue, to be farmed out to the highest bidder. Additionally, venison, timber and other forest products were at the king's disposal - whether as concessions to loyal courtiers or sold as cash commodities. How far this was true in the Norman period is difficult to estimate, due to lack of reliable records. In the forests, too, the king asserted his will in an arbitrary way, not in accordance with the common law as it evolved in the twelfth century.[100] This enabled his officers to deal severely with poachers, and also to

---

98 Clanchy, *England and its Rulers*, 75; Frame, *The Political Development of the British Isles*, 101.

99 Clanchy, *England and its Rulers*, 55; *The course of the Exchequer by Richard, son of Nigel*, ed. and transl. C. Johnson (London, 1950), 60.

100 *The Course of the Exchequer*, 59-60.

take drastic action against lurking outlaws, who habitually took refuge in forest areas. And the forest was emotive not only for the outlaw, but also for the king himself. As leader of a hunting party, he conveyed a powerful image of authority, one which harked back to time beyond memory.[101]

Successful royal government tempered its authoritarian bias with an element of popular appeal - aimed at the people who mattered. One overtly popular strand lay in citation of 'the law of King Edward' - a reminder that the Norman kings claimed to be his legitimate successors. It was no accident that both Henry I and Stephen married kinswomen of King Edward.[102] From the reign of William I, the Norman kings stressed their title as 'King of the English' - in contrast to their English predecessors who simply styled themselves king. Citation of English customary law helped to blur the legal distinction between French and English.[103]

But assimilation did not reach up to the highest level in one important area where it could have furthered the interests of the monarchy. The cults of royal saints served a valuable political purpose in the pre-Conquest centuries. After 1066, whereas the incoming French higher clergy were quick to perceive the continued value of these cults for the claims of their monasteries, the new

---

101 Clanchy, *England and its Rulers*, 55.

102 Brooke, *The Saxon and Norman Kings*, 191.

103 George Garnett, "'Franci et Angli'": the legal distinctions between peoples after the Conquest', *Anglo-Norman Studies VIII*, ed. R. Allen Brown (Woodbridge, 1986), 111, 136.

royal house saw no political potential in them.[104] Nor
was readiness to utilize the 'law of King Edward' matched
by royal enthusiasm for the cult of the king whose legitimate successors the Norman rulers claimed to be, even
though Westminster abbey, adjacent to the royal palace,
assiduously promoted this cult from the time of Abbot
Gilbert Crispin (1085-1117/18).[105]

The Norman kings inherited from Edward a system of
government which was effective, intelligent and sophis-
ticated, and itself inspired by late Carolingian practice.[106]
After the Conquest, Englishmen in the lower ranks of
the government hierarchy continued to manage the administration along former lines. It has been argued that
the gradual disappearance of these men, whether through
death or retirement, caused an administrative crisis in
the years around 1100, when their expertise vanished
with them. Instances of what previous generations of
scholars claimed as new administrative experiments can
be depicted alternatively as misunderstood and make-
shift efforts to prop up a system which was collaps-

---

104 Susan J. Ridyard, *The Royal Saints of Anglo-Saxon England: a
study of West Saxon and East Anglian cults* (Cambridge, 1988),
250-1.

105 Emma Mason,'"The Site of King-Making and Consecration":
Westminster Abbey and the Crown in the Eleventh and Twelfth
Centuries', *The Church and Sovereignty: Essays in Honour of Michael
Wilks*, ed. Diana Wood, Studies in Church History Subsidia 9 (Oxford,
1991, 64-6.

106 James Campbell, *Essays in Anglo-Saxon History* (London, 1986),
170.

ing.[107] The pre-Conquest language of government was English, but after a short experiment with bilingual documents early in the reign of William I, the use of English was allowed to lapse and Latin became the sole language of government.[108] The meaning of a Latin text was clear to every trained clerk, who could translate it into whichever vernacular his employer preferred to use. For although Englishmen were removed from politically-sensitive offices such as that of sheriff, many remained in a lower managerial capacity. But the dropping of English as a language of government meant that the accumulated corpus of official documents in the vernacular became obsolete, leading to the loss, through unintelligibility, of a working archive.[109]

On the other hand, the reigns of the Norman kings witnessed the emergence and development of the royal chancery, the king's central writing office. Developments can be traced tentatively from the reign of William I, and with confidence from that of Henry I.[110] The reigns of the Norman kings witnessed a steady increase in the volume of documentation produced by clerks of the royal court. The number of surviving documents issued in the king's name throughout successive reigns rises constantly,

---

107 W.L Warren 'The Myth of Norman Administrative Efficiency', *Transactions of the Royal Historical Society*, fifth series, 34 (1984), 113-32.

108 M.T. Clanchy, *From Memory to Written Record: England 1066-1307* (London, 1979), 165.

109 *Ibid.*, 19.

110 Campbell, *Essays in Anglo-Saxon History*, 177.

the output doubling every two or three decades. Precise totals for any reign, or any regnal year, cannot now be known, owing to subsequent losses. It has been suggested that the surviving charters represent about 1% of the total which were issued. Developments in England reflect a wider trend throughout Western Europe, as popes and secular rulers developed their administrations.[111] To the extent that this rising output of royal missives reflected administrative orders, the increase should have reflected a tightening of the control exercized by the Norman kings over their subjects, and petitions for letters of protection, or of rectification of injuries caused by neighbours, indicate a belief in the powers at the king's disposal. But the very fact that a considerable proportion of the kings' affluent subjects petitioned for redress of wrongs committed by others or requested special exemptions or privileges, suggests also that in practice royal government was less all-pervasive than the growing number of mandates might suggest. The number of surviving royal letters per regnal year throughout Stephen's reign overall is double that for the reign of William Rufus. The latter was a much more assertive ruler but he lived at a time when documentation of the royal will was less usual than it later became. Even so, the Norman kings as a whole are known to have issued a much higher output of written mandates than their rivals the kings of France. Petitioners were increasingly prepared to pay rulers for a written guarantee of their rights, something which may reflect a growing faith in the power of the written word as much as the growing effectiveness of royal government. The Anglo-Norman output

---

111 Clanchy, *From Memory to Written Record*, 42-4.

was lower than that of the Papacy,[112] although the Papal mandates reflected activities throughout much of Europe. To the extent that their growing numbers indicate an increasingly assertive papal administration, this in turn helps explain the strong resistance of the English kings towards the extension of canon law jurisdiction in England, with its destabilizing effects upon royal sovereignty.

The Norman kings also used the written word to record their own rights and assets - as in the case of Domesday Book and its antecedent documentation, and also in that of the Pipe Rolls, which are known to have been kept from some uncertain date in the reign of Henry I.[113] The recording of royal rights gave the kings an advantage over their subjects, who were slow to follow suit. But enthusiasm for record-keeping outran techniques of using an archive systematically, and Domesday Book was perhaps quickly relegated to being a symbol of royal omniscience rather than a working tool.[114]

Given the recent debate concerning the use of documentation by the later Anglo-Saxon kings, and the likelihood of the loss of their archive after the Norman Conquest, it cannot be argued with certainty that the Norman kings were the first rulers of England to issue written instructions authenticated with the royal seal, (as distinct from the charters of privilege which the Anglo-Saxon kings

---

112 *Ibid.*, 46.

113 *Ibid.*, 108-122.

114 *Ibid.*, 55, 121-2.

certainly granted), but the balance of the evidence lies in this direction.[115] In this sense the clerks of the Norman kings rendered their masters' rule more effective than that of their English predecessors.

This contrast must not be laboured, owing to the limitations which still persisted for decades, indeed for generations, in the methods and functions of royal record-keeping. The Pipe Rolls were essentially concerned with money owed to the king, and it was a long time before records were kept in any detail of the terms on which concessions and privileges were granted by the crown. The king's subjects, and notably clerical proprietors, took advantage of the lack of royal records of concessions, and energetically devised their own versions of rights conceded by the crown. Monastic forgeries survive from later eleventh century England, but their numbers increased sharply in the early decades of the twelfth century, with the growing perception of the value of documentation of rights and privileges. Hopeful petitioners presented such documents for authentication, at a price, by the imposition of the royal seal. Vigilant chancery staff rejected the more outrageous claims to privileges and exemptions, but without an archive against which they could check these lengthy lists, some royal rights were inadvertently conceded. Occasionally a scribe employed by the king was persuaded by a clerical petitioner to draw up a convincing-looking charter which included more alleged royal concessions than former rulers had in fact conceded. When this was presented for confirmation, it would have a good chance of being ratified, given

---

115 *Ibid.*, 121.

the scribe's distinctive handwriting and knowledge of official formulae.[116]

In later Anglo-Saxon England a royal seal, which authenticated documents issued in the king's name, was already in use, but it is likely that early seals were destroyed by the unfolding of missives. From the reign of Edward the Confessor, seals were attached in such a way as to leave them intact after opening the document - so that their attachment would authenticate its contents. The new manner of attaching the seal meant that it was now produced with a design on both sides, like the *bullae* of the Popes and the Byzantine and German emperors, while the magisterial image of the king was copied from that of the Ottonian ruling dynasty in Germany.[117] The Norman kings continued the practice of authenticating documents in this way - and also followed Edward in using the seal to project an imposing image of majesty, with ensuing designs reflecting various artistic traditions.[118] The seal of William Rufus, for instance, echoes on one face the equestrian image his father had used as duke of Normandy, while the majesty side, which depicted the enthroned king, is reminiscent of representations of earlier English rulers. Through the distribution of documents authenticated by the royal seal, therefore, the king publicized an image of himself both as the aggressive warrior and as the triumphant sovereign. The seal of

---

116 *Ibid.*, 252.

117 G. Heslop, 'Seals', in Zarnecki, Holt and Holland, eds., *English Romanesque Art*, 298; 301, no. 328.

118 *Ibid.*, 300.

William Rufus is also the first surviving English seal to describe the ruler as king 'by the grace of God', a phrase which perhaps derived from German seals.[119] These words conveyed the concept that the ruler's authority had Divine sanction, as a result of his anointing. A similar point was conveyed with the introduction, on two successive seal-types of Henry I, of a bird which may represent the Holy Spirit on the orb of the seated ruler, while elements of his crown reflect Byzantine models.[120] The royal brothers were, therefore, using the images on their seals to impress upon their subjects that their authority was both sacrosanct, and 'imperial', in that they did not recognise the jurisdiction of an earthly overlord, or any restraint on the scope of their authority.

The Norman kings inherited from their English predecessors a strong monetary system. This was reinforced by the policy of ordering regular recoinages, when existing coins were ordered to be exchanged for the new type, enabling the king to take a percentage from the exchange-rate. Throughout any one reign, the changing designs could be used by the ruler to make specific political points, which he knew would be grasped, literally, by virtually all of his subjects.[121] In the early generations of Norman rule, many of the moneyers, the men charged with oversight of coin-production in the localities, were of English or Anglo-Danish ancestry, thus promoting

---

119 *Ibid.*, 302, no. 329.

120 *Ibid.*, 302, no. 330.

121 Marion Archibald, 'Coins', in Zarnecki, Holt and Holland, eds., *English Romanesque Art*, 321-2, 327-8, nos. 392-3, 396; 329, no. 410; 335, no. 439.

some continuity of practice.[122]

Stabilization of the weight of the coinage was determined by William the Conqueror, establishing the heav-
ier-weight silver penny, with its 'sterling' quality.[123] Coin-
dies were distributed on royal authority from a central
point, so that the coinage had a uniform appearance. The
names of the moneyers working at the various regional
mints appeared on the coins, so that it would be known
who was responsible for the quality of output in each
locality. But keeping tabs on all concerned was no easy
task. There were times in the reign of Henry I when the
quality of production, and more especially its bullion
content, failed to come up to standard.[124] There was a
short-term break-down around 1108, then a recovery,
followed by a more serious deterioration which prompted
Bishop Roger of Salisbury to order the mutilation of the
moneyers, which, according to the chroniclers, occurred
at Christmas 1124. But the names of some of these moneyers continued to appear on the coins, and it is recorded
on the Pipe Roll of 1130 that several moneyers escaped
this purge.[125] And yet savage punishment of the defaul-
ters seemed called for, since the king's mercenary troops
were rendered discontented during a crucial campaign
by being paid in light-weight coins.

---

122 *Ibid.*, 326-7, nos. 387-8, 390.

123 *Ibid.*, 320.

124 *Ibid.*, 321, nos. 411-12.

125 *Ibid.*, 332, no. 421. See also *The Anglo-Saxon Chronicle*, ed.
and transl. Whitelock *et al.*, 191, annal for 1125.

VIII

Visual images of majesty, which helped to reinforce the political message of the king's authority, were important in an age when visual symbols impressed more people than did the written word. Royal fortresses, such as the Tower of London, had a serious military and political purpose, but their presence also dominated the skyline and towered over the much lower profiles of civic, commercial, or domestic buildings. Lavish expenditure on castles both reinforced the king's political grip on his lands, and symbolized it. The same symbol of majesty was conveyed in royal projects of a civil nature, notably in the rebuilding of Westminster Hall by William Rufus,[126] or the great abbey churches: Reading, built on the orders of Henry I, and Faversham, founded by Stephen.[127] All these buildings had one overt purpose (whether as the setting for a crown-wearing, as at Westminster, or as royal mausolea, in the case of the churches), and also an unspoken, but equally important one, which was to depict the power and majesty of the king who could commission such projects. We cannot recapture the spectacular impression created by those buildings as they existed in their prime, but their visual impact upon the subjects of the Norman kings should not be underestimated.

The impact of the public appearance of any of these

---

126 Clanchy, *England and its Rulers*, 25-6; Zarnecki, Holt and Holland, eds., *English Romanesque Art*, 147, 154-6.

127 Zarnecki, Holt and Holland, eds., *English Romanesque Art*, 147-8.

rulers is even more difficult to gauge. Their Byzantine-inspired regalia was worn only on ceremonial occasions, yet they had also to create an impression on their subjects as they travelled around, from day to day. Some slight indication of their everyday finery can be glimpsed from the contents of the tomb in Winchester cathedral which may have been that of William Rufus. These included fragments of precious materials, including gold tissue and other luxury fabrics, together with remnants of jewellery and a fragmented boar-spear. There was also a fine dragon-head of walrus ivory - perhaps the handle of a knife or dagger.[128]

With visual propaganda went literary propaganda. William I commissioned works of literature favourable to himself. No work of this kind now survives from the reign of William Rufus, although there may be traces of some such lost work in his favourable portrayal by the twelfth-century writer Geoffrey Gaimar.[129] Queen Edith Matilda probably commissioned the favourable portrayal of her English royal ancestors which appears in William of Malmesbury's *Deeds of the Kings of the English*, while her successor, Queen Alice, the second wife of Henry I, owned a work on the deeds of Henry I which its

---

128 *Ibid.*, 216, no. 186; J. Beckwith, *Ivory Carving in Early Medieval England*, (London, 1972), no. 54; J.G. Joyce, 'On the opening and removal of a tomb in Winchester Cathedral reputed to be that of King William Rufus', *Archaeologia*, 42 (1869), 309-21. See also Clanchy, *England and its Rulers*, 19.

129 Emma Mason, 'The Hero's Invincible Weapon: an aspect of Angevin Propaganda, *The Ideals and Practice of Medieval Knighthood III*, ed. C. Harper-Bill and Ruth Harvey (Woodbridge, 1990), 125. See also Clanchy, *England and its Rulers*, 26.

author set to music.[130] A favourable, indeed heroic, image was essential for any ruler who wanted to attract a powerful military following - something which contributed to the success of William Rufus.[131] Conversely no ruler could allow himself to become the object of hostile, and even worse, jeering remarks, hence the savage treatment meted out by Henry I to an incautious jongleur who composed lampooning verses about him.[132] A king had to deal harshly with dissidents if he was not to lose credibility, and Stephen's misfortunes were caused to a large extent by his kindness towards his adversaries.[133] His Norman predecessors were successful because they knew when to be tough. William the Conqueror matured amidst violence and knew the value of being seen to be firm, and even ruthless.[134] His two immediate successors learned that lesson - and were able to build on his achievement. Harsh rule was perceived by their subjects as bringing more stability, for more people, by and large, than Stephen's softer approach. And effective rulers were respected even where they were disliked. The personal names of the men of the Norman ruling dynasty quickly became the most popular ones bestowed on their English subjects. And since the single most common recorded

---

130 Mason, 'The Hero's Invincible Weapon', 125.

131 Clanchy, *England and its Rulers*, 68-9.

132 Hollister, *Monarchy, Magnates and Institutions*, 300.

133 Clanchy, *England and its Rulers*, 125.

134 Brooke, *The Saxon and Norman Kings*, 145-6.

name was William, this reflects something of the stature of those kings, as perceived by their people.[135]

---

135 Clanchy, *England and its Rulers*, 57.

FURTHER READING

There are several excellent recent surveys of the Anglo-Norman period, including:

Frank Barlow, *The Feudal Kingdom of England 1042-1216* (London, 4th edn. 1988).

Marjorie Chibnall, *The World of Orderic Vitalis* (Oxford, 1984).

Marjorie Chibnall, *Anglo-Norman England 1066-1166* (Oxford, 1986).

Michael Clanchy, *England and its Rulers 1066-1272; Foreign Lordship and National Identity* (London, 1983).

Carolly Erickson, *The Medieval Vision: Essays in History and Perception* (Oxford, 1976).

Robin Frame, *The Political Development of the British Isles 1100-1400* (Oxford, 1990).

Pauline Stafford, *Unification and Conquest, a Political and Social History of England in the tenth and eleventh centuries* (London, 1989).

Translations of the major primary sources for the reigns of the Norman Kings are printed in *English Historical Documents II. 1042-1189*, ed. D.C. Douglas and G.W. Greenaway (second edn., London, 1981).

Individual texts, published with introductions and parallel English translation, include:

Marjorie Chibnall's invaluable edition and translation of *The Ecclesiastical History of Orderic Vitalis*, 6 vols.,

(Oxford, 1969-80).

Gesta Stephani, ed. and transl. K.R. Potter, introd. R.H.C. Davis (Oxford, 1976).

The Historia Novella by William of Malmesbury, transl. and ed. K.R. Potter (London, 1955).

Monographs on the reigns of the individual kings include:

D.C. Douglas, *William the Conqueror; the Norman Impact upon England* (new edn. London, 1969).

Frank Barlow, *William Rufus* (London, 2nd edn., 1990).

R.H.C. Davis, *King Stephen 1135-1154* (3rd edn. Harlow, 1990).

H.A. Cronne, *The Reign of Stephen 1135-54: anarchy in England* (London, 1970).

Christopher Brooke, *The Saxon and Norman Kings* (2nd edn., 1967), provides a stimulating introduction.

Government and administration are covered in:

Michael Clanchy, *From Memory to Written Record: England 1066-1307* (London, 1979).

Judith A. Green, *The Government of England under Henry I* (Cambridge, 1986).

W.L. Warren, *The Governance of Norman and Angevin England 1086-1272* (London, 1987).

Relations between the Norman kings and other rulers are discussed by:

John Le Patourel, *The Norman Empire* (Oxford, 1976).
W.E. Kapelle, *The Norman Conquest of the North. The Region and its Transformation 1000-1135* (London, 1979).
G.W.S. Barrow, *The Anglo-Norman era in Scottish History* (Oxford, 1980).
R.R. Davies, *The Age of Conquest. Wales 1063-1415* (Oxford, 1991).

Relations between church and state are discussed in:

Frank Barlow, *The English Church 1066-1154* (1979).
M. Brett, *The English Church under Henry I* (Oxford, 1975).

and in studies of individual clerics, including those by:

Margaret Gibson, *Lanfranc of Bec* (Oxford, 1978).
R.W. Southern, *Saint Anselm: a Portrait in a Landscape* (Cambridge, 1990).
Edward J. Kealey, *Roger of Salisbury, viceroy of England* (Berkeley, 1972).

Art and artefacts of the period are discussed and splendidly illustrated in *English Romanesque Art 1066-1200,* ed. G. Zarnecki, Janet Holt and T. Holland (London, 1984).

Studies in aspects of the economic and social history of the period are published in *Domesday Studies: papers read at the Novocententary Conference of the Royal Historical Society and the Institute of British Geographers, Winchester, 1986*, ed. J.C. Holt (Woodbridge, 1987).

The most comprehensive coverage of recent research on the Anglo-Norman period is published in an ongoing annual series, which began as *Proceedings of the Battle Conference on Anglo-Norman Studies*, ed. R. Allen Brown (Vols. I - IV, 1979-82) and continued as *Anglo-Norman Studies*, vols. V-XI, 1983-89, ed. R. Allen Brown; Vol. XII, 1990 - ed. Marjorie Chibnall.

Volumes of the collected articles of leading medievalists, on specific aspects of the Anglo-Norman period, which have earlier appeared in various scholarly journals include the following:

Frank Barlow, *The Norman Conquest and Beyond* (London, 1983).
R. Allen Brown, *Castles, Conquests and Charters: Collected Papers* (Woodbridge, 1989).
R.H.C. Davis, *From Alfred the Great to Stephen* (London, 1991).
D.C. Douglas, *Time and the Hour: some collected papers* (London, 1977).
C. Warren Hollister, *Monarchy, Magnates and Institutions in the Anglo-Norman World* (London, 1986).

BIBLIOGRAPHY OF THE WRITINGS OF EMMA MASON.
1975 - 1991

Abbreviations

BIHR	*Bulletin of the Institute of Historical Research*
JEH	*Journal of Ecclesiastical History*
JMH	*Journal of Medieval History*
MH	*Medieval History*
MP	*Medieval Prosopography*
RR	*Rutland Record*
SCH	*Studies in Church History*

BOOKS AND ARTICLES

1975

'English Tithe Income of Norman Religious Houses', *BIHR* 48, 91-4.

'The Resources of the Earldom of Warwick in the Thirteenth Century', *Midland History* 3, 67-75.

1976

'The Mauduits and their Chamberlainship of the Exchequer', *BIHR* 49, 1-23.

'Maritagium and the Changing Law', *BIHR* 49, 286-9.

'The Role of the English Parishioner 1100-1500, *JEH* 27, 17-29.

1977

'William Rufus: Myth and Reality', *JMH* 3, 1-20

1978
'Timeo Barones et Dona Ferentes', *Religious Motivation*, ed. D. Baker, (*SCH* 15, Oxford), 61-75.

1979
'A Truth Universally Acknowledged', *The Church in Town and Countryside*, ed. D. Baker (*SCH* 16, Oxford), 171-86.

1980
The Beauchamp Cartulary: Charters 1100-1268, (ed.), Pipe Roll Society, new series 43.
'The King, the Chamberlain and Southwick Priory', *BIHR* 53, 1-10.
'Magnates, Curiales and the Wheel of Fortune: 1066-1154', *Proceedings of the Battle Conference on Anglo-Norman Studies II. 1979*, ed. R. Allen Brown (Woodbridge), 118-40, 190-5.

1981
'Through a Glass Darkly: sources and problems in English Baronial Prosopography', *MP* 2:2, 21-31.

1982
'Pro Statu et incolumnitate regni mei: royal monastic patronage 1066-1154', *Religion and National Identity*, ed. S. Mews (*SCH* 18, Oxford), 99- 117.
'Rocamadour in Quercy above all other churches: the healing of Henry II', *The Church and Healing* ed. W.J. Sheils (*SCH* 19, Oxford), 39-54.

1984
'Legends of the Beauchamps' ancestors: the use of baro-

nial propaganda in medieval England', *JMH* 10, 25-40.
'St. Wulfstan's Staff: a legend and its uses', *Medium Aevum* 53, 157-79.

1985

'Westminster Abbey's Rutland Churches: 1066-1214' *RR* 5, 163-6.
'Healing Shrines in Medieval England', *Catholic Medical Quarterly* 36, 130-7.

1986

'Change and Continuity in eleventh-century Mercia: the experience of St. Wulfstan of Worcester, *Anglo-Norman Studies VIII*, ed. R. Allen Brown (Woodbridge), 154-76.

1987

'Lords and Peasants in medieval Rutland: the Rutland estates of the Mauduit chamberlains of the Exchequer' *RR* 7, 236-41.
'The Donors of Westminster Abbey Charters; c.1066-1240', *MP* 8:2, 23-39.

1988

Westminster Abbey Charters 1066-c.1214, (ed.), with the assistance of the late Jennifer Bray, continuing the work of the late Desmond J. Murphy (London Record Soc., 25).
'Fact and Fiction in the English Crusading tradition: the earls of Warwick in the twelfth century', *JMH* 14, 81-95.

1990

St. Wulfstan of Worcester c.1008-1095 (Oxford, 1990).

'Westminster Abbey and the Monarchy between the reigns of William I and John (1066-1216)', *JEH* 41, 199-216.

'The Hero's Invincible Weapon: an Aspect of Angevin Propaganda', *The Ideals and Practice of Medieval Knighthood III*, ed. C. Harper-Bill and Ruth Harvey (Woodbridge), 121-37.

1991

'William Rufus and the Historians', *MH* 1:1, 6-22.

'Saint Anselm of Canterbury: philosopher, theologian and tactician', (rejoinder), *MH* 1:2, 152.

'"The Site of King-making and consecration": Westminster Abbey and the Crown in the eleventh and twelfth centuries', *The Church and Sovereignty: essays in honour of Michael Wilks*, ed. Diana Wood (*SCH* Subsidia Oxford), 9, 57-76.

'Westminster Abbey and its Parish Churches', *Monastic Studies II*, ed. Judith Loades, (Bangor, 1991).

'Henry I : Decoding an Enigma', *MH* 1:3.